GW00367569

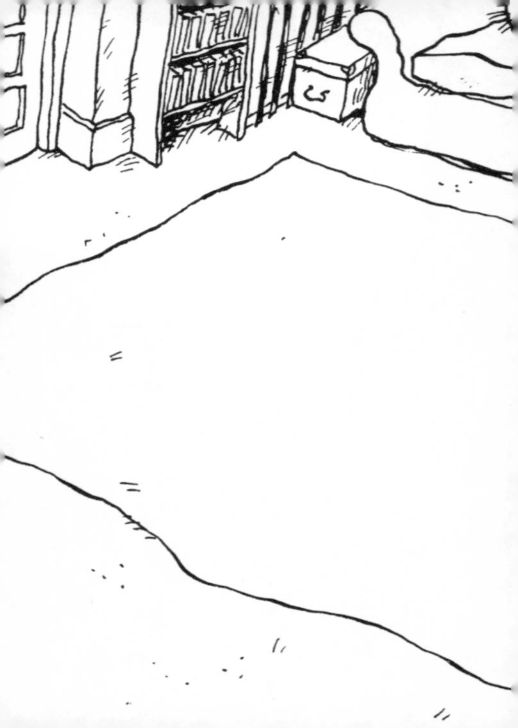

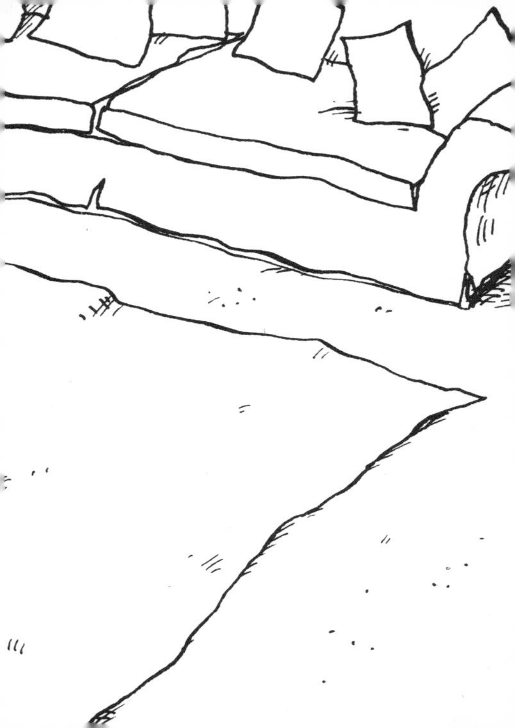

WHAT BABIES DO:

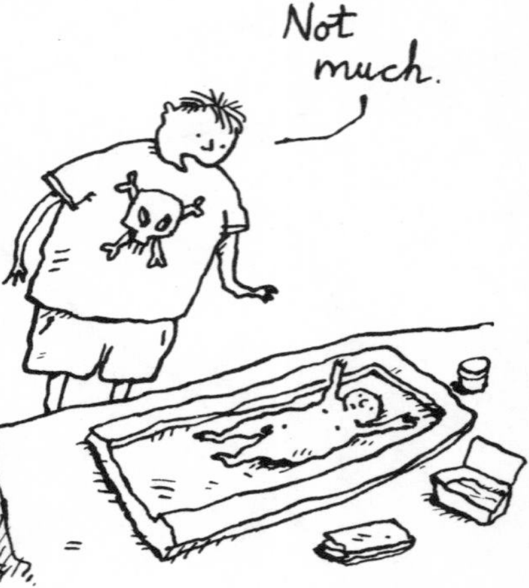
Not much.

The
SECRET THOUGHTS
of
BABIES

Waaaaaaaaaaa...

Steven Appleby

First published in 1996
This paperback edition published 2001

Copyright Steven Appleby © 1996

The moral right of the author
has been asserted.

Bloomsbury Publishing PLC
38 Soho Square, London W1D 3HB

ISBN 0 74 75 5855 8

Printed in Italy by
Editoriale Johnson SpA

FOR JASPER & CLEMMIE

THE COMPLETE
NEW-BORN BABY
RANGE OF ACTIVITY:

Asleep.

Awake.

Eating.

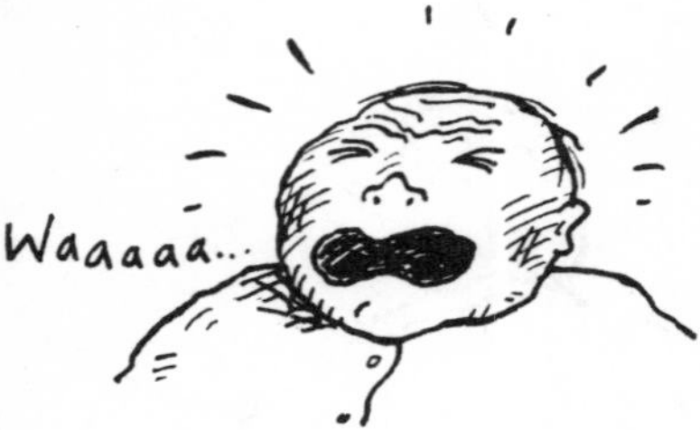
Waaaaa...

Cross.

Not cross.

(NB – Babies are never
happy. Just not cross).

Filling a nappy.

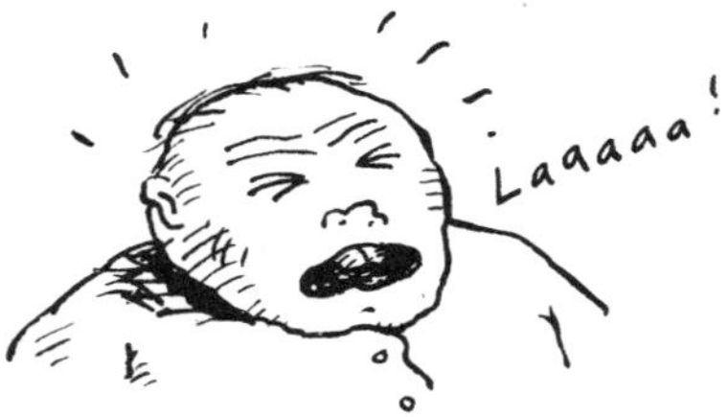
Laaaaa!

Hungry.

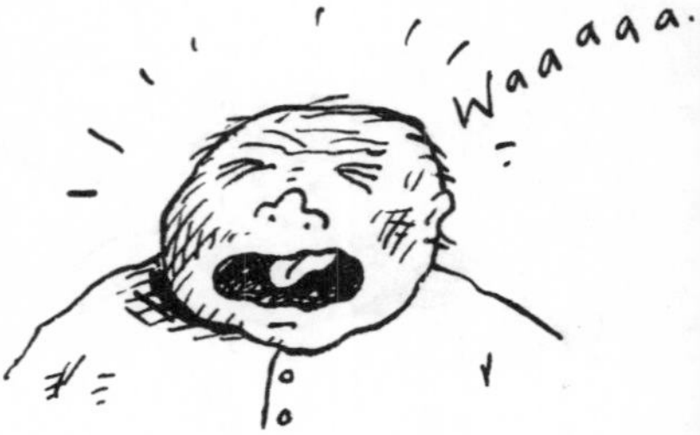
Waaaaa.

Windy.

A BABY'S ABILITY TO EMPATHISE WITH OTHER LIVING CREATURES:

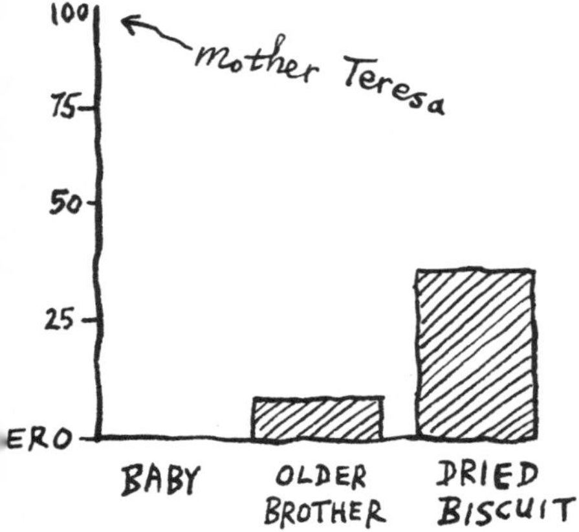

100
mother Teresa
75
50
25
ERO
BABY
OLDER BROTHER
DRIED BISCUIT

SOME ADVICE ~
ALWAYS SUPPORT YOUR
BABY'S HEAD...

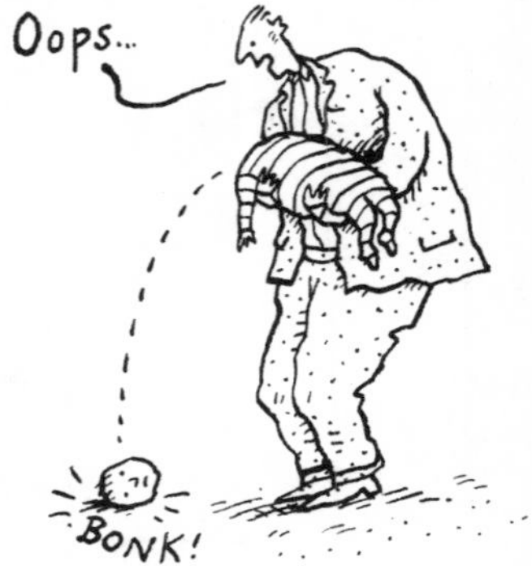
Oops...
BONK!

OR THIS WILL HAPPEN.

THOUGHTS AT 3 ~ 4 WEEKS

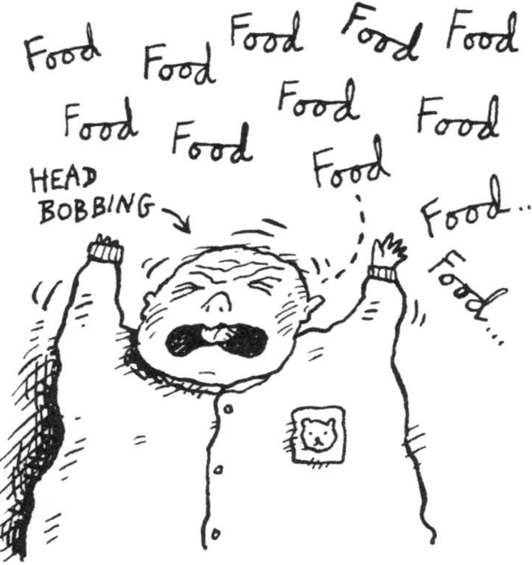

HOW BABIES SEE
THE WORLD

fig a.

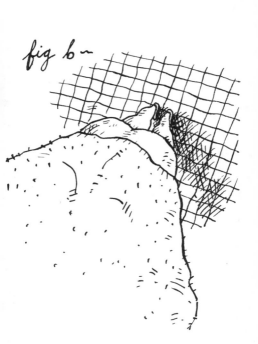

fig 6~

fig c –

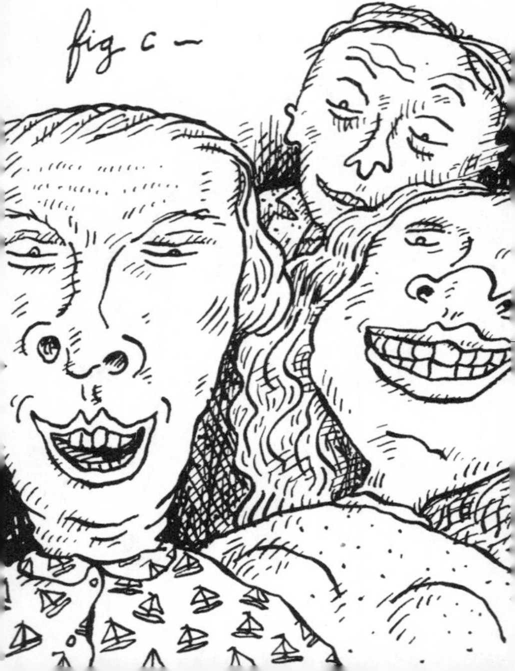

4 - 10 WEEKS

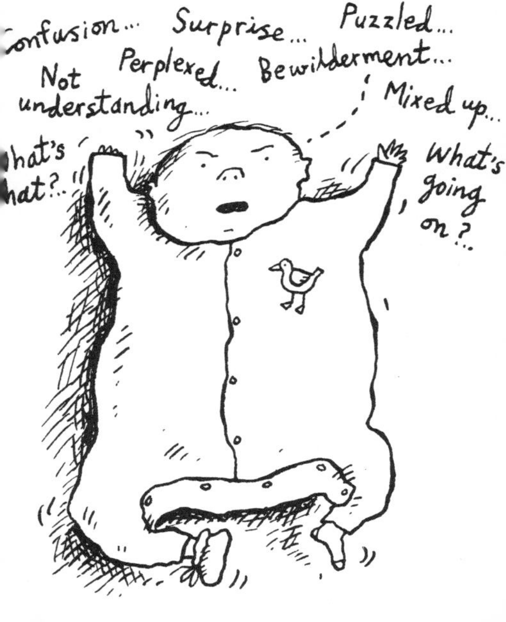

onfusion...
Surprise...
Puzzled...
Not understanding...
Perplexed...
Bewilderment...
Mixed up...
hat's hat?..
What's going on?..

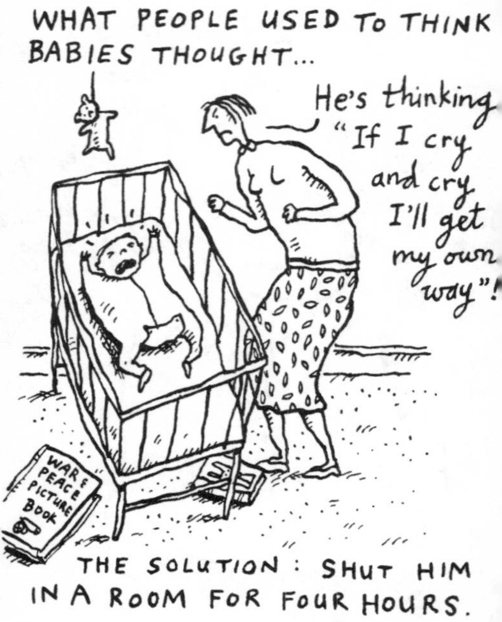
WHAT PEOPLE USED TO THINK BABIES THOUGHT...
He's thinking "If I cry and cry I'll get my own way"!
WAR & PEACE PICTURE BOOK
THE SOLUTION: SHUT HIM IN A ROOM FOR FOUR HOURS.

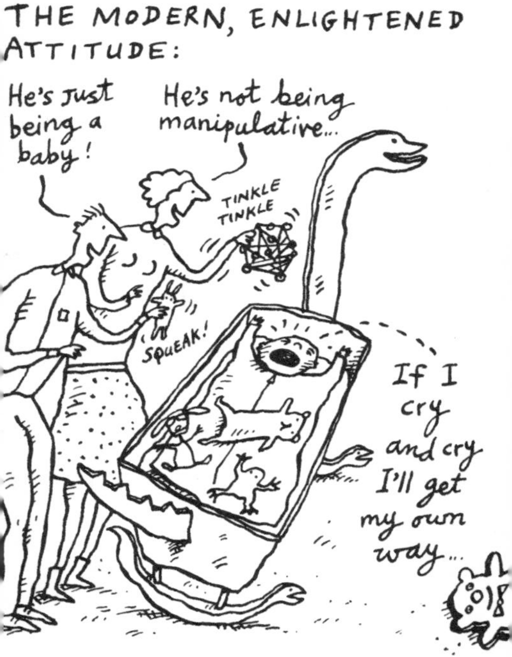
THE MODERN, ENLIGHTENED ATTITUDE:
He's just being a baby!
He's not being manipulative...
TINKLE TINKLE
SQUEAK!
If I cry and cry I'll get my own way...

THINGS THAT UPSET BABIES

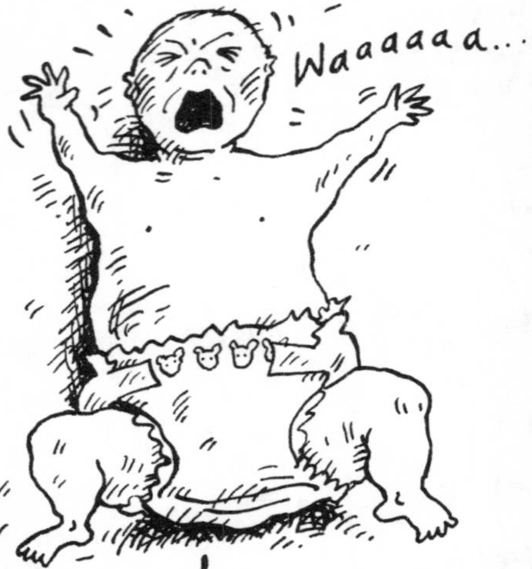
Waaaaaa...

Having their nappy changed.

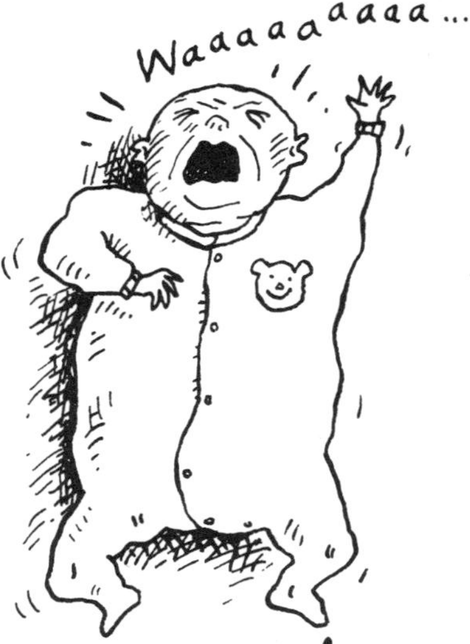
Waaaaaaaaaa...

Not having their nappy changed.

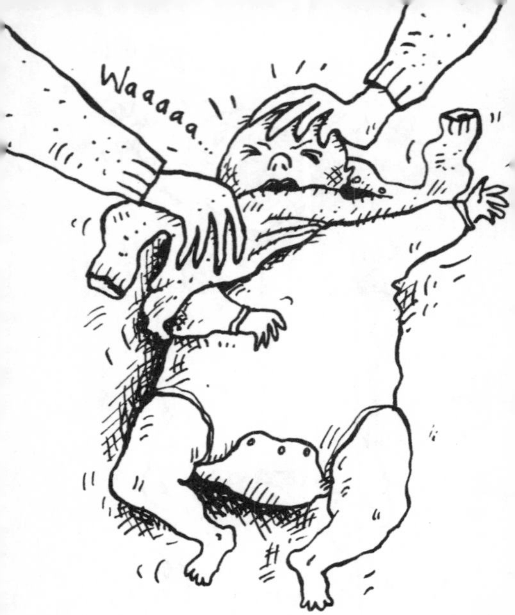
Waaaaa...

Being dressed.

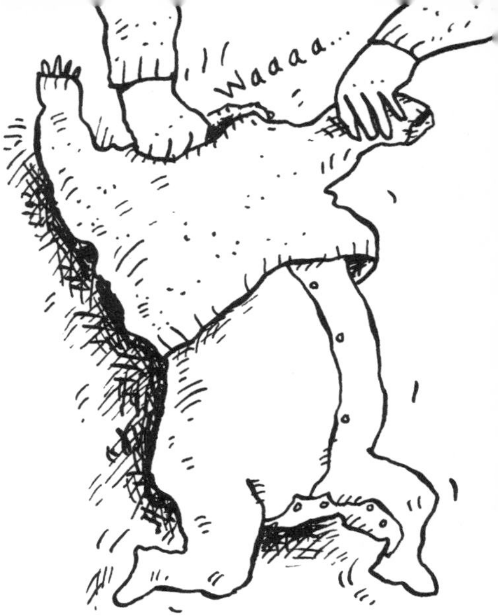
Waaaa...

Being undressed.

THINGS THAT MAKE BABIES HAPPY...

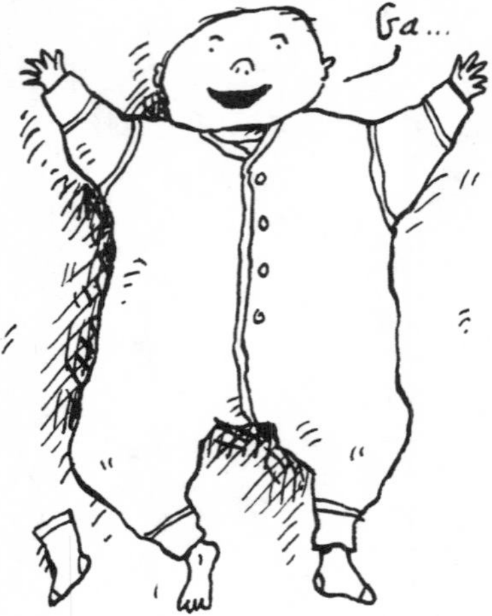
Ga...

Food.

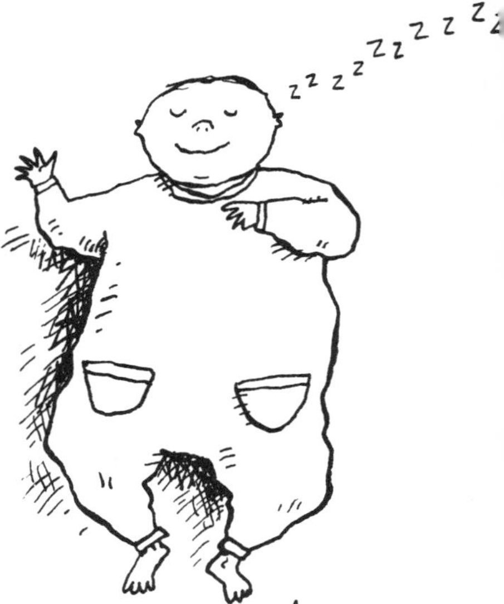
z z z z z z z z z z z z z

Being asleep.

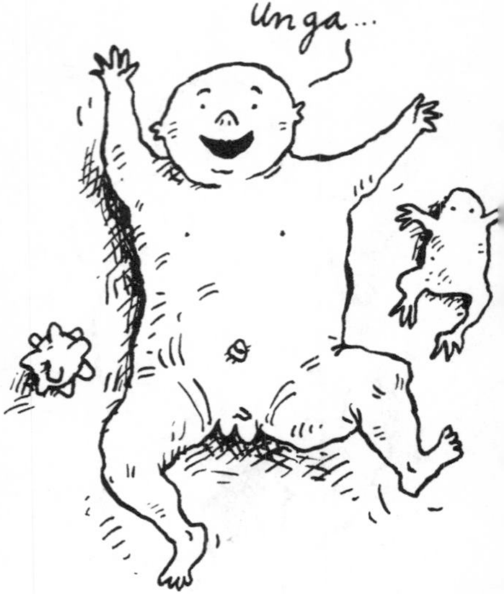
Unga...

No clothes on at all.

SOME BABY THOUGHTS

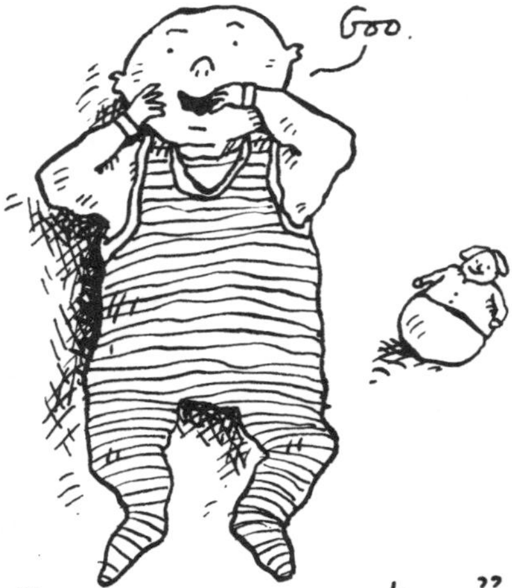
Goo.

"In a moment..."

" ... for no particular reason, I am going to throw my arms and legs in the air and scream and scream and scream.

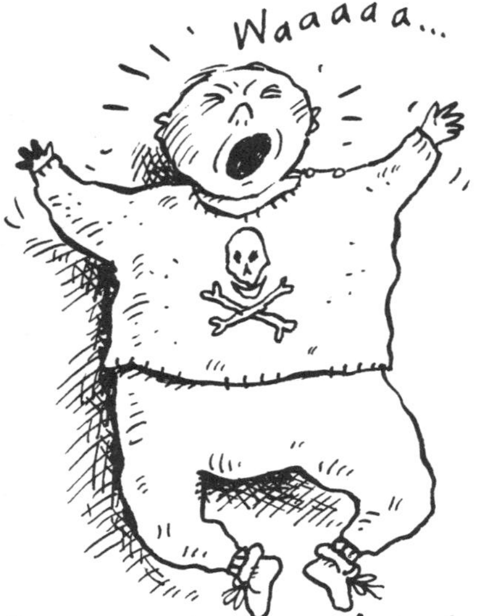
Waaaaa...

"I am doing this to drive you utterly crazy."

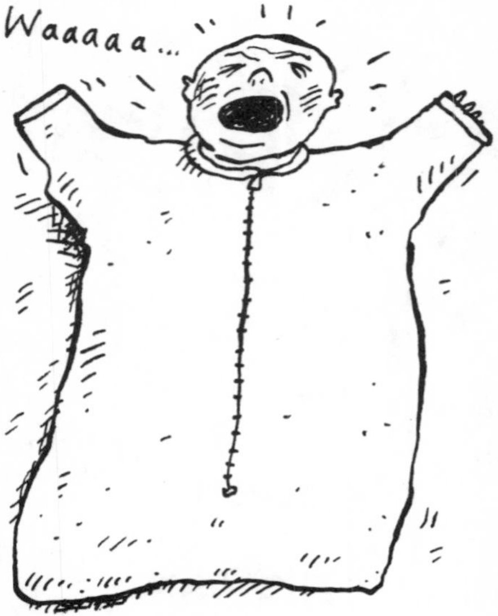
Waaaaa...

"I could stop at any time - if I wanted to."

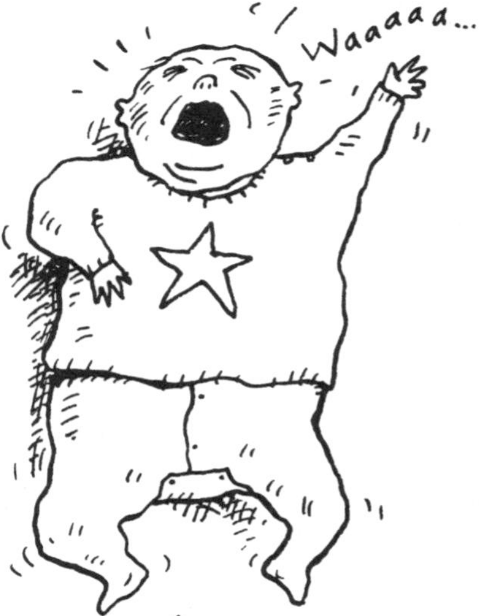
Waaaaa...

"I'm unhappy so I want you to be unhappy too."

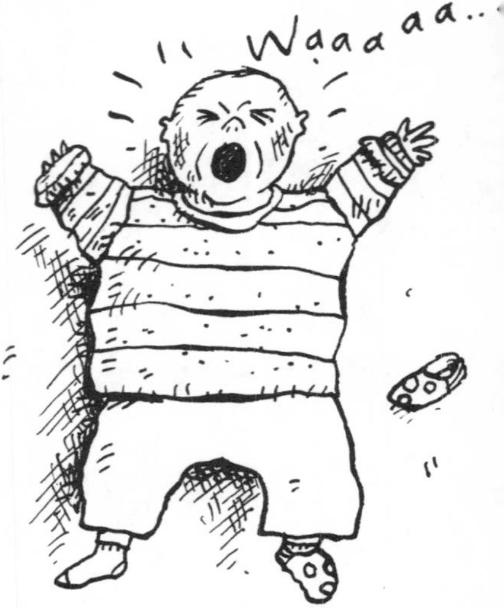
Waaaaa...

"I'm testing you to see how much you love me."

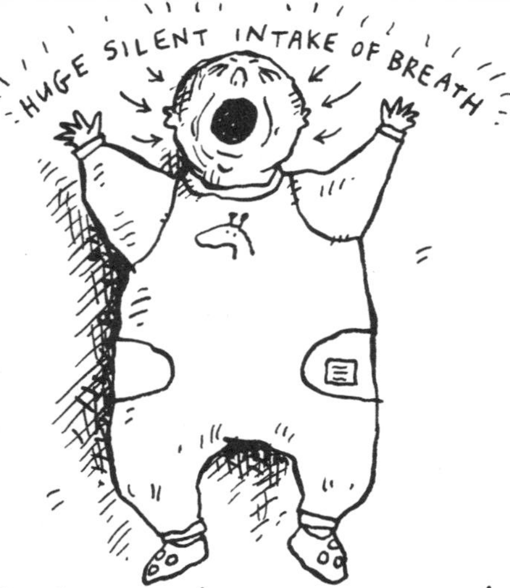
HUGE SILENT INTAKE OF BREATH

"There's been a mistake! I'm not your baby! The hospital mixed up. Please send me home..."

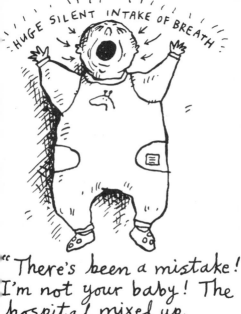

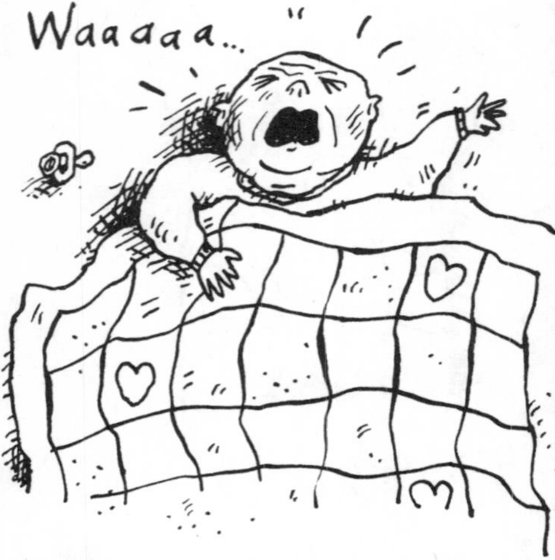
Waaaaa...

"I WON'T go to sleep!!"

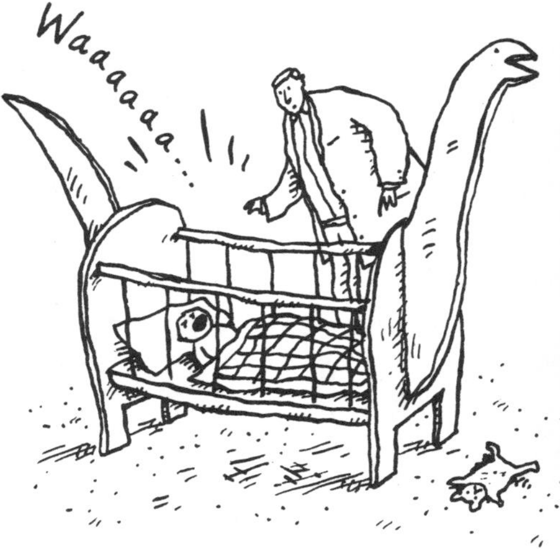

"I won't go to sleep here..."

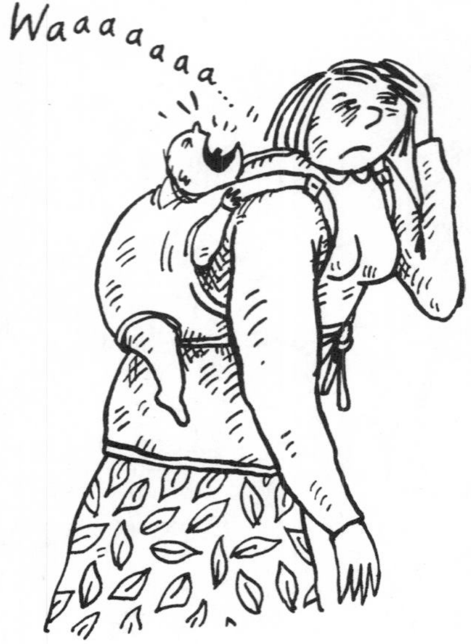

"or here..."

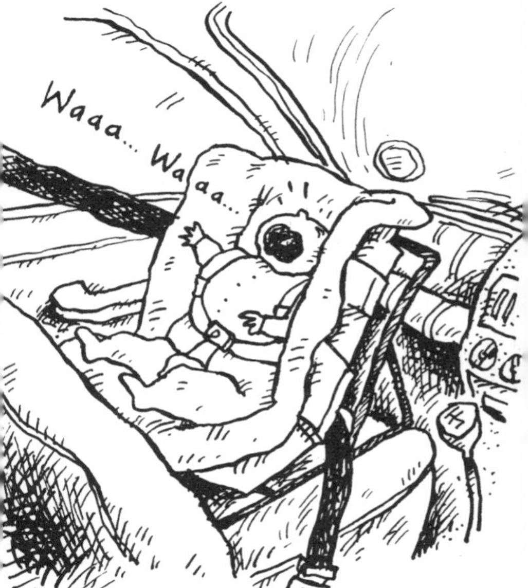
Waaa... Waaa...

" or here... "

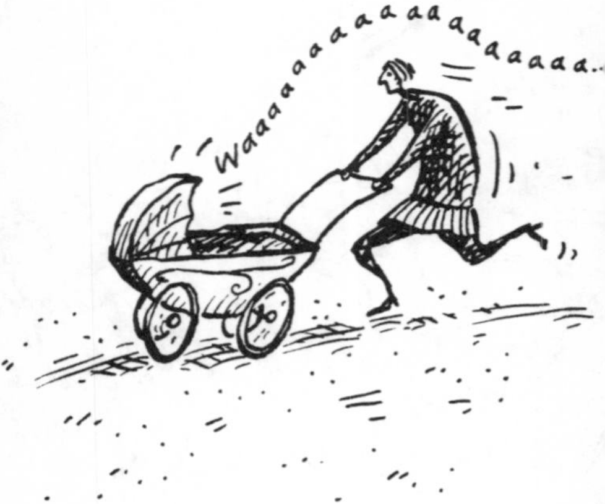
Waaaaaaaaaaaaaaaaaaaaa..

"or here..."

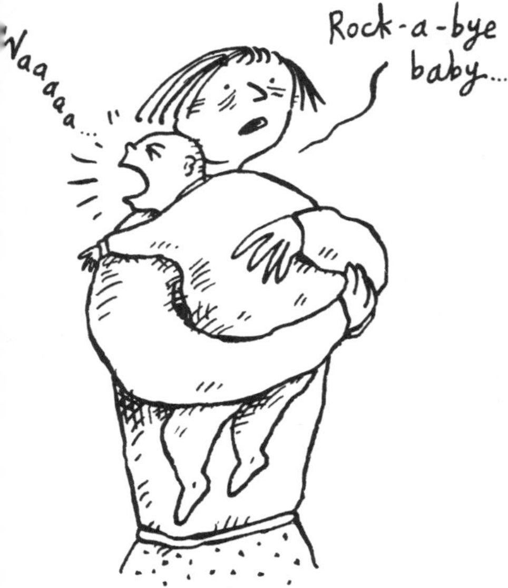

"or here..."

AT LAST...

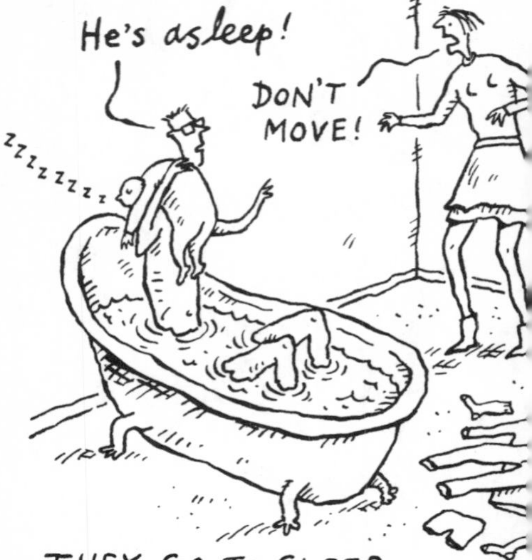
He's asleep!
DON'T MOVE!

THEY GO TO SLEEP IN AWKWARD PLACES.

THEY SLEEP TOO QUIETLY...

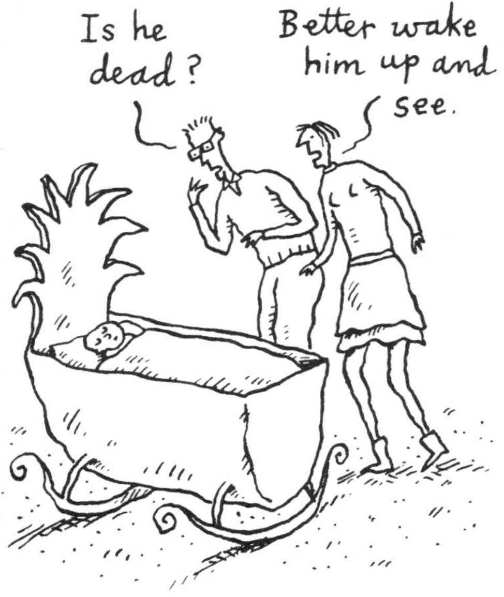
Is he dead?
Better wake him up and see.

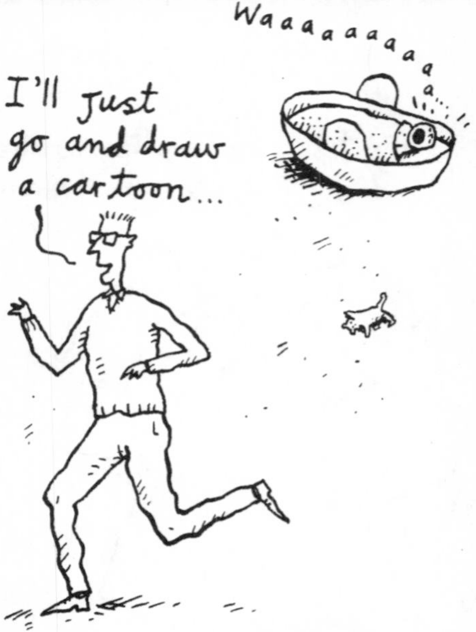
Waaaaaaaaaa...
I'll Just go and draw a cartoon...

AS SOON AS YOU'RE BUSY THEY WAKE UP.

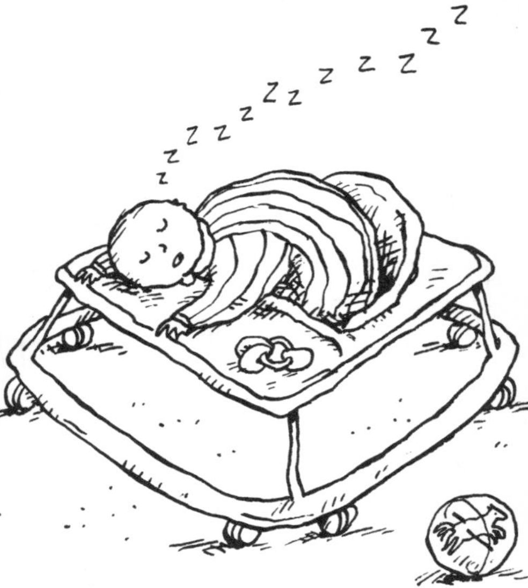

THEY SLEEP DURING THE DAY SO THEY CAN STAY AWAKE <u>ALL</u> <u>NIGHT</u>!

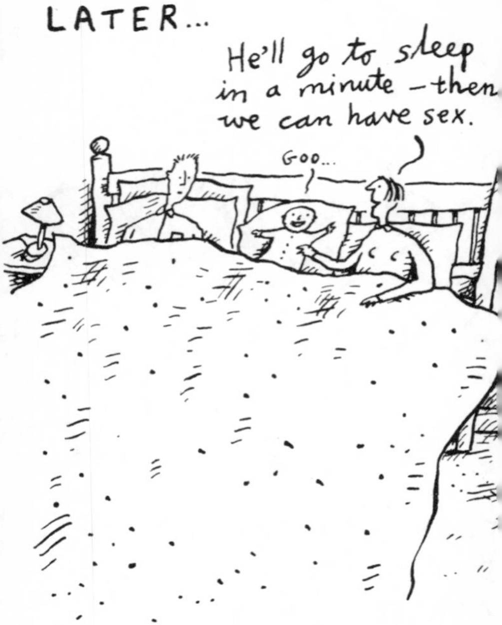
LATER...
He'll go to sleep in a minute – then we can have sex.
GOO...

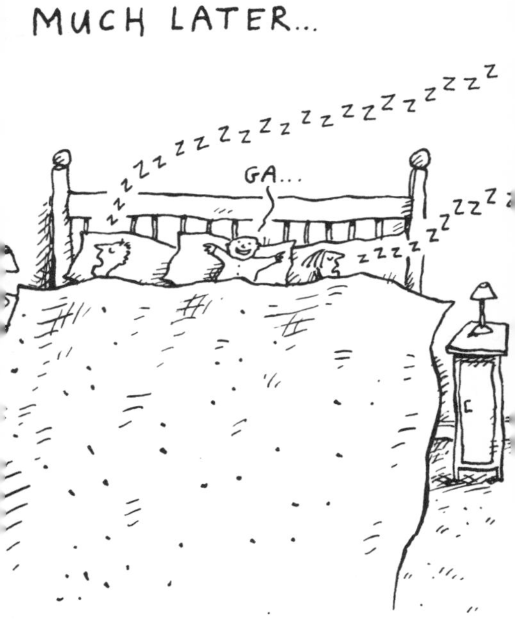
MUCH LATER...
GA...

MORE BABY THOUGHTS

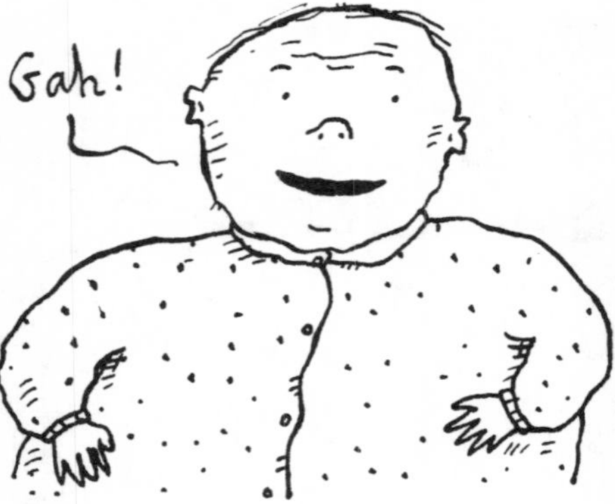

Gah!

"I have filled my nappy with green slime."

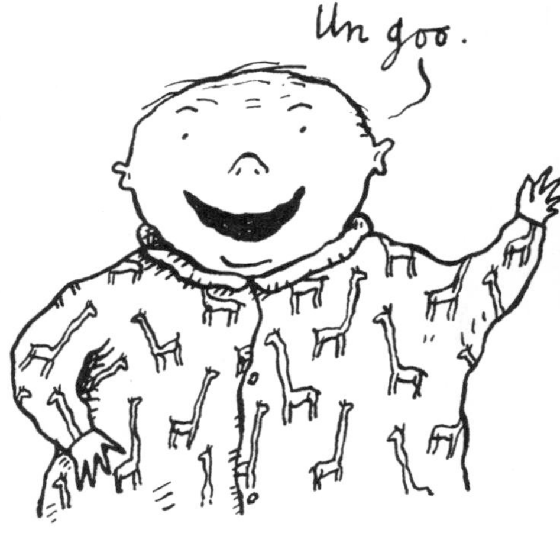
Un goo.

"The parent name I learn to say first is the one I love most"

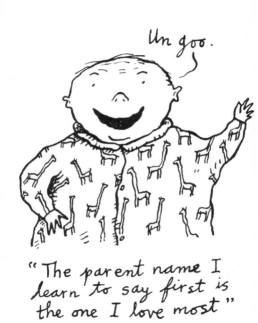

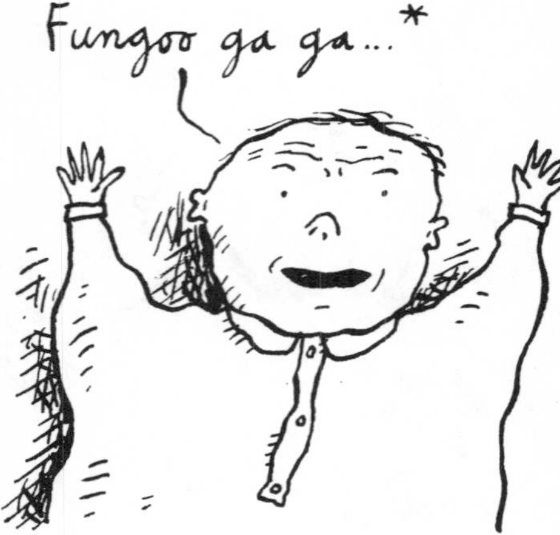
Fungoo ga ga...*

* "Please answer this vital question which has been preying on my mind..."

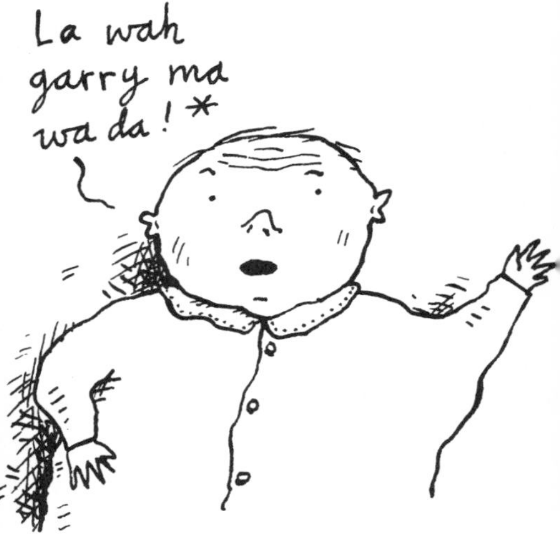

* "Am I adopted?"

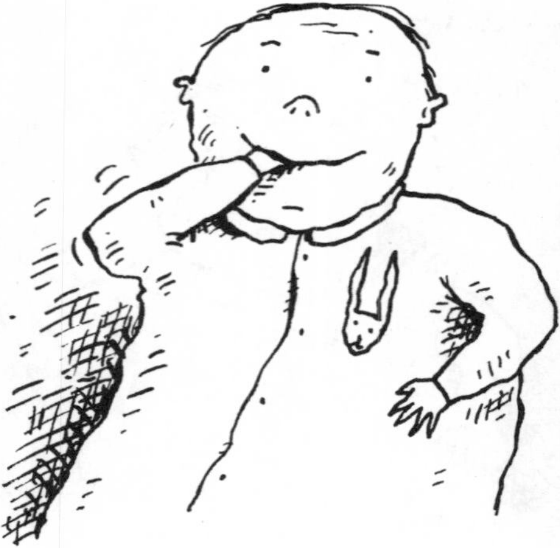

"I am about to be sick."

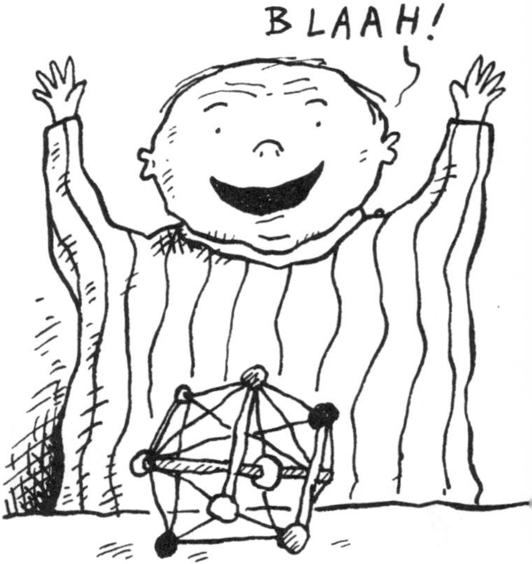
BLAAH!

"I LOVE this toy!"

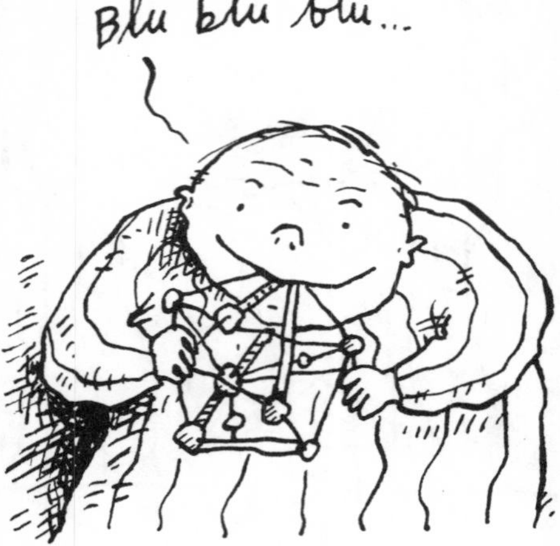
Blu blu blu...

"It's my favourite..."

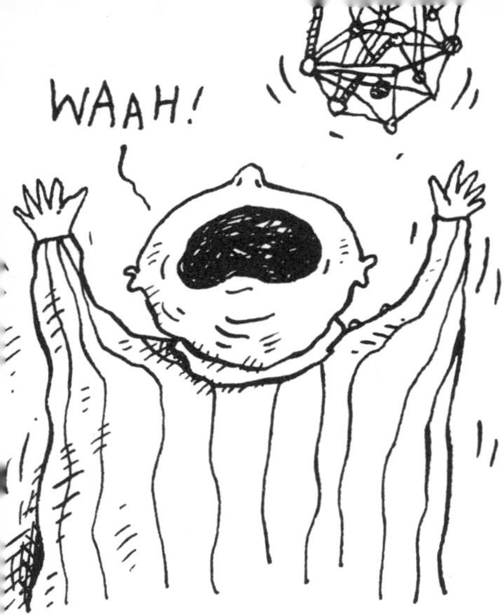

"Now I HATE it!!"

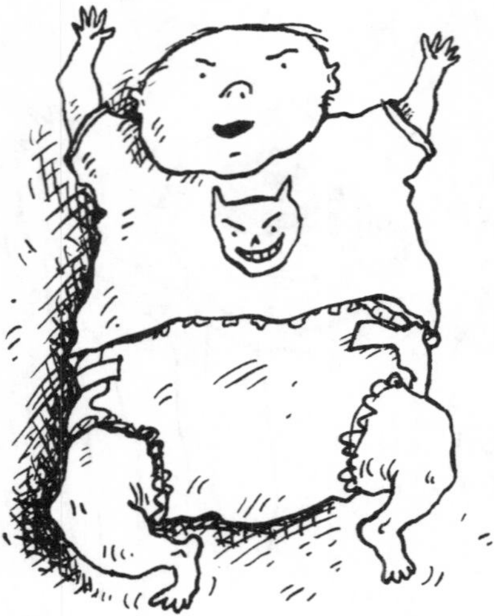

"Am I the Meaning of Life?.."

IT IS HARD TO BELIEVE, BUT ONE DAY YOUR BABY WILL GROW UP...

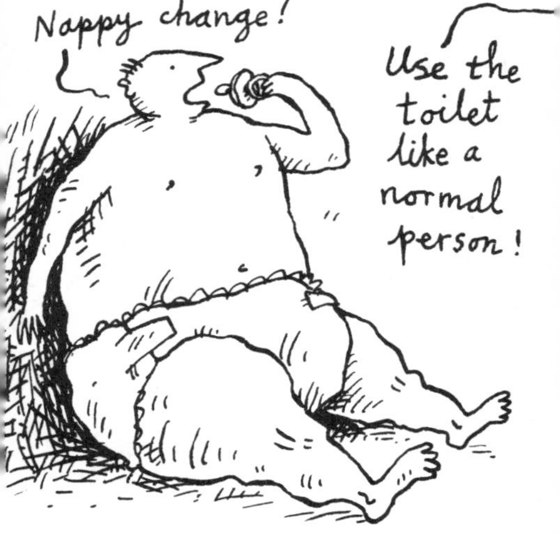
Nappy change!
Use the toilet like a normal person!

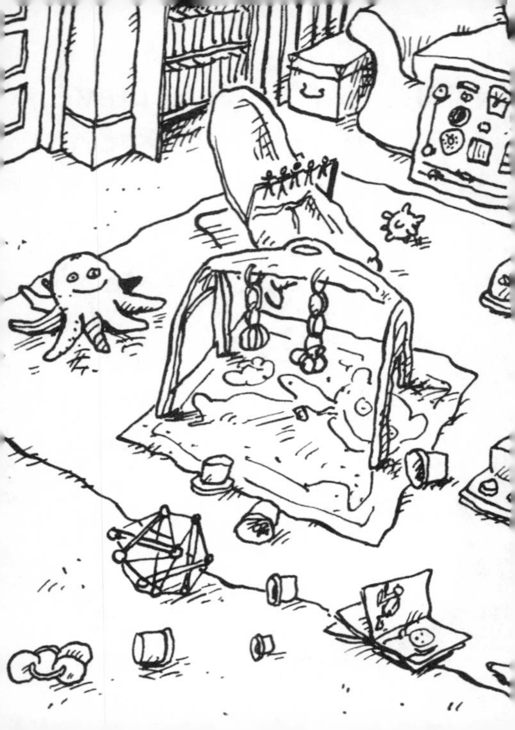

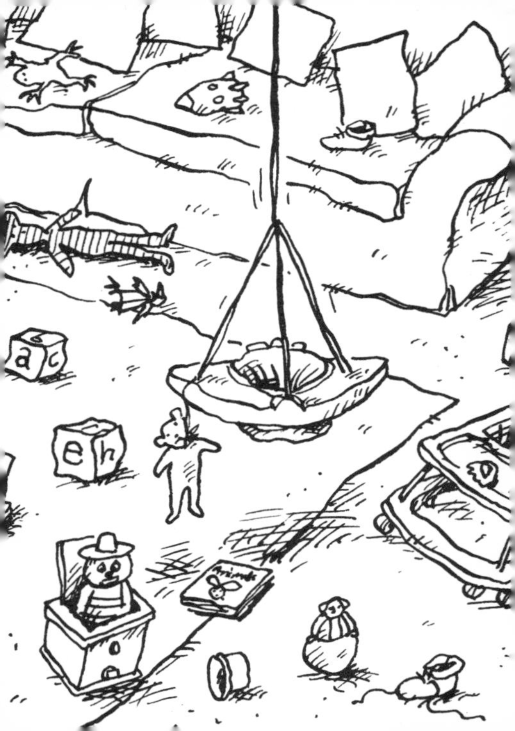
a
c
e
h
Animals